Service, Stewardship & Stress

Service, Stewardship & Stress

Jack Crabtree
Kevin Flannagan
Mark Oestreicher
Neil Wilson
Len Woods

*David R. Veerman,
Series Editor*

VICTOR BOOKS

A DIVISION OF SCRIPTURE PRESS PUBLICATIONS INC.
USA CANADA ENGLAND

TOPICS AVAILABLE IN FLEX SESSIONS

Friendship, Tough Times & God's Will
Success, Pride & a Sex-Crazed Society
Dating, Identity & Bible Study
Sex, the Future & Prayer
Handling Emotions, Church, Money & Stuff
Service, Stewardship & Stress
Witnessing, Family & Moral Choices

Scripture, unless otherwise indicated, is taken from the *Holy Bible, New International Version*®. Copyright © 1973, 1978, 1984 by International Bible Society. Used by permission of Zondervan Publishing House. All rights reserved. Verses marked TLB are taken from *The Living Bible,* © 1971, Tyndale House Publishers, Wheaton, IL 60189. Used by permission. All rights reserved.

Copyediting: Daryl Lucas
Cover Design: Mardelle Ayres

ISBN: 1-56476-139-8

CONTENTS

About the Authors

The authors of **Flex Sessions** are youth ministry veterans, having written and led, collectively, thousands of meetings for high school and junior high young people. These lessons come out of their experiences and creativity.

JACK CRABTREE
Executive Director
Long Island (New York) Youth for Christ

KEVIN FLANNAGAN
Director
East Alabama Area Youth for Christ

MARK OESTREICHER
Junior High Pastor
Calvary Church, Santa Ana, California

NEIL WILSON
Pastor
Eureka (Wisconsin) United Methodist Church

LEN WOODS
Pastor to Students
Christ Community Church, Ruston, Louisiana

Flex Sessions are produced in cooperation with The Livingstone Corporation, David R. Veerman, Editor. The authors would like to thank Tim Atkins, Claudia Gerwin, Michael Kendrick, and Daryl Lucas for their assistance during the writing of this book.

HOW TO USE
FLEX SESSIONS

Actually, the whole point of **Flex Sessions** is that you can use them any way you want! Here are a few options to get you started.

The Topics

- Teach all 12 sessions for a balanced quarter's worth of material.
- Promote each topic as a mini-series during the summer or as a change of pace in your regular program.
- Build a retreat around the four sessions of one topic.

Options within the Session

- Use them as they're written for high school students, or follow the adaptations for junior high/middle school.
- Follow the material in **bold type** as a guideline for those times when you'll be doing the talking.
- Extend a session with the Additional Ideas if you have more time available.
- Replace an activity with one from the Additional Ideas if you see one your group would love.
- Use the Active Bonus ideas if your setting permits high-energy activities.

Clip Art

- Make a calendar to post or send home, picturing each of the upcoming sessions.
- Photocopy one illustration onto 3" x 5" cardstock along with the time, place, and a brief description of the meeting, and send as a promotional postcard.
- Make postcards to let absent kids know they're missed — and what they're missing.
- Add clip art to the reproducible charts and handouts in the sessions.
- Brighten your bulletin board with illustrations.
- Novelty printers can make T-shirts, hats, 3-ring binders, and just about anything else you might want to use as attendance incentives, give-aways to visitors, or mementos of retreats, etc.
- Don't forget the reduction/enlargement feature if your photocopier has one.

Whether you teach **Flex Sessions** just as they're written, or pick and choose from the options above, you'll find that **Flex Sessions** give you the resources you need for the flexibility you want.

SERVICE

ONE

Join the Revolution

KEY CONCEPT:	Unselfish love
BIBLE PASSAGE:	Matthew 6:1-4
OBJECTIVE:	As a result of this meeting, students will know how to touch others' lives without drawing attention to themselves.
MATERIALS CHECKLIST:	☐ Bibles ☐ Pencils or pens ☐ Newsprint for walls ☐ Felt-tip pens ☐ Incomplete sentences (Starters) ☐ Some semblance of a Santa Claus outfit (Action): a beard, a belly, a belt, a bellow (ho ho ho), a red coat would be nice too ☐ Stuff for Santa's sack: a clock, a wallet, a book, a pen, a phone, a paper plate, a roll of cellophane tape or a tube of glue, a hammer, a wash cloth, a food can, a felt-tip pen set, car keys, a camera
JUNIOR HIGH/MIDDLE SCHOOL ADAPTATION:	Early adolescence is a time of self-centeredness as students focus on their own needs and problems. Christian students need to understand that they should be looking for ways to be kind to others. This lesson should work well with junior highers as written with the following adaptations. After ''Graffiti,'' begin with ''Act Out'' (Active Bonus) instead of ''Finish the Sentence.'' Then, during Study, instead of small groups, have individual students read the sentences from Jesus' words.

STARTERS

(10 min.)

"Graffiti"

Before the meeting starts, cover one wall with (blank) newsprint. Have a few helpful/challenging phrases already written on it, such as: "The only problem with a living sacrifice is that it keeps crawling off the altar"; "When you pray, you'll get everything you really kneed"; "Jesus is Lord of all or not Lord at all"; etc.

In a prominent spot on the paper write: "Practice random kindness and senseless acts of beauty!"

As kids enter the room, give them felt-tip pens and encourage them to cover the wall with similar phrases—phrases that challenge people to do unselfish acts of kindness. (If you sense that they will need help thinking of phrases, tell them to recall some of the statements that have challenged them to be kind.)

To start, briefly discuss what their favorite phrases are, and why. Then use the Transition below (skipping "Finish the Sentence").

"Finish the Sentence"

Photocopy the following incomplete sentences, or distribute paper and dictate the phrases. Tell everyone to finish the sentences. Keep the papers anonymous.

● "Another word for kindness is _____."

● "Jesus demonstrated kindness by _____
_____."

● "One person with whom (or one situation where) I could be kinder is _____
_____."

● "I really know I'm serving when _____
_____."

Collect the papers and read aloud what students wrote for the first two sentences. Then spend a couple of minutes discussing what true kindness is.

First, ask one or two volunteers to tell whom they need to be kinder to, and why. Then ask everyone to give examples of kindness they've seen or received.

Transition

As a transition, ask: **Why is being kind sometimes so difficult to do?** (Because it isn't always cool.)

Some people regard kindness as a weakness; they belittle, ignore, or even mock kind acts because they think that strong, capable people don't do kind things. This can become a real barrier to anyone who cares about what those people think.

Point out that—as the study will show—being genuinely kind actually takes a great deal of courage.

STUDY
(25 min.)

Bible Study

Divide into six groups. Assign each group a sentence or phrase from Jesus' words in Matthew 6:1-4, broken down like this:

1. 6:1a—"Be careful not to do your 'acts of righteousness' before men, to be seen by them."
2. 6:1b—"If you do, you will have no reward from your Father in heaven."
3. 6:2a—"So when you give to the needy, do not announce it with trumpets, as the hypocrites do in the synagogues and on the streets, to be honored by men."
4. 6:2b—"I tell you the truth, they have received their reward in full."
5. 6:3-4a—"But when you give to the needy, do not let your left hand know what your right hand is doing, so that your giving may be in secret."
6. 6:4b—"Then your Father, who sees what is done in secret, will reward you."

Ask each group to prepare an explanation of what Jesus meant, with an example, if possible. Have each group share its explanation.

Here are some possibilities:

6:1a—Don't do good deeds just for show or to get people to notice.
6:1b—If you do something just to impress others, the recognition you get will be your only reward—you will miss out on a heavenly reward.
6:2a—People who call attention to their good deeds are hypocrites—inside they're not really good; they're merely trying to gain points with others.
6:2b—If you toot your horn, that's all the reward you should expect for your good deeds.
6:3-4a—As much as possible, hide your good deeds; don't even brag to yourself.
6:4b—God promises to reward every good deed done in secret.

After discussing their findings, say something like: **So Jesus has a special category for the good things we do that no one else seems to notice. God does see and remember everything, and He promises to reward us. And this can be fun; in fact, sometimes the greatest fun we can have is doing good when no one else can see us!**

CHALLENGE
(5 min.)

Talk To

Continue: **A few years ago a unique, challenging statement began to catch on. No one seems to know who said it first. I wrote the statement** on the wall earlier: **"Practice random kindness and senseless acts of beauty!"** The phrase has encouraged a lot of people to go out in the world trying to do good things in sneaky ways, helping people without getting caught! They are trying to put into practice what Jesus said: **Do good quietly and for no selfish reason at all!**

Explain that you have a special guest who will give them tools to use as they go out and practice random kindness and senseless acts of beauty.

ACTION

(5 min.)

"Santa Cause"

This will take some planning ahead and a little extra time, but it will be well worth the investment.

Have someone enter the room dressed like Santa Claus. (This does not have to be elaborate or even terribly accurate—just a reasonable approximation of Santa.) Explain that this is a very special Santa with a very special Cause. Over his shoulder he has slung his "Serving Sack," filled with presents. Everyone who wants to participate in a project of showing kindness to others will be given a present by Santa. Then, during the next week, they must use their items to serve someone.

The presents should include a clock, a wallet, a book, a pen, a phone, a paper plate, a roll of cellophane tape or a tube of glue, a hammer, a washcloth, a food can, a felt-tip pen set, car keys, a camera, and/or anything else you can substitute.

Tell students to be prepared to report next week on what they did. (Include yourself in this exercise to set the example and build in some motivation.)

Here are some true "random kindnesses and senseless acts of beauty" that you can use as examples:

- After a snowstorm, late at night, several kids organized a guerrilla shoveling crew and visited some homes of the elderly and cleaned their walks.
- Someone sent flowers to the high school principal's secretary.
- Someone paid the toll for four strangers behind him when traveling on the tollway.
- Someone arranged to buy milk for everyone in the school cafeteria one day at lunch.

ACTIVE BONUS

"Act Out"

Divide into groups of two or three. Have each group draw one of the words listed below out of an envelope. Explain that their task is to think through and then silently act out (pantomime) a short scene depicting that word in action.

Allow time for preparation; then have the groups act out their scenes (words) one at a time.

Here are the words to use: rude, abusive, inconsiderate, selfish, mean, obnoxious, pushy, obstinate.

Afterward, ask what the words have in common. Explain how each one was a way that people are unkind to each other. Then ask: **If that's unkindness, what is kindness?**

ADDITIONAL IDEAS

"Making Points"

Play a game of volleyball as an object lesson. Explain that a team can only score points when it *serves*. Obviously, therefore, the server really makes a difference on the team. Ask if there are any other parallels to the Christian life and making a difference in the world. To make the game more interesting, change the rules a bit: allow no spiking and require each team to have at least five different players hit the ball before sending it over the net.

"Field Trip"

Announce that you are going to take a field trip to a large, nearby department store, perhaps to do some shopping. Before you go, however, have everyone draw the name of a character (described below) out of an envelope. Explain that everyone should try to experience the store as the character they have drawn.

Here are some characters: a poor person; a person who is very depressed; a very sad person; a lonely person; an angry person; a lost child; someone who is sick; (use others if you like).

It would be good to have a wheelchair or two for kids to use, so that they can better experience the store from the point of view of a person who cannot walk.

Spend no more than 15 minutes doing this.

Is That a Need I See?

KEY CONCEPT:	Helping people with needs
BIBLE PASSAGE:	Matthew 25:31-46; James 2:14-17
OBJECTIVE:	As a result of this meeting, students will learn to be more sensitive to the needs of others and to how they can help.
MATERIALS CHECKLIST:	☐ Bibles ☐ One copy of the "Role Plays" worksheet Active Bonus ☐ Serving tray ☐ Garbage bag ☐ Miscellaneous items for the "At Your Service" relay (a cotton ball, a paper cup, a rock or paperweight, a book, a spoon, a toothpick, a Ping-Pong ball, a pencil, a golf ball, a napkin, a salt shaker, etc.)
JUNIOR HIGH/MIDDLE SCHOOL ADAPTATION:	Certainly early adolescents need to be challenged to help the needy, so this lesson is very appropriate. During "Handy Helpers," however, be sure to have adults supervise each small group, giving direction and ideas as they design their machines. Under Study, push students to be very specific about where to find needy people in the community and what they can do to help meet those needs. Also, make sure the "Role Play" doesn't drag on too long, and try to choose actors you think will not merely goof off playing their parts.

STARTER

(15 min.)

"Handy Helpers"

In this activity, groups of kids design and act out "Rube Goldberg" machines. Divide into groups. Explain that some people want to help others without getting involved directly. The task of each group, therefore, is to create a machine that will deliver some help to a needy person with the operator of the machine only having to pull a lever or push a button. Everybody in the group has to be some part of the group's machine. Then have each group draw the description of a needy person out of an envelope. The needy people could include: a homeless person needing shelter or warmth; a hungry person needing food; a lonely person needing a friend; a sick person needing medical care; a mother needing someone to baby-sit her children; and so forth.

Allow time for the groups to create their machines; then have each group set up and operate its machine, one at a time. Afterward discuss what people actually do to help others in need without getting personally involved. These could include: hiring someone else; giving money; expecting the government to do the work; talking or writing about the problem; etc.

STUDY

(20 min.)

Discussion

Explain that the Book of James was written by Jesus' half-brother, James. Then have a student read aloud James 2:14-17. Then ask:

- **What does James mean?** (Real faith in God leads us to doing good deeds for others.)
- **What quality of faith is James emphasizing?** (Real, sincere faith; not superficial lip service)
- **What happens when a person just says nice things instead of really helping someone?** (The spoken words add insult to the lack of help.)

Explain that James refers to "a brother or sister without clothes and daily food." Ask: **In our community, who fits that description? How would we find out about someone whom we could help?**

Note: Potential sources of information include: the police department, the high school office, a pastor, a local food pantry, and social workers. Be sure to warn students that once they know of someone's need, they are responsible to do something to help meet that need if possible.

In balance, also point out that your students can't meet all the world's needs single-handedly. They must focus on needs that they can actually do something about, not ones out of their control or beyond their ability to affect. Some needs are major and require many people working together to meet them; other needs can be met more simply by individuals acting alone out of God's love.

Most people—including most students—bump into others with simple needs every day—needs that your students can help with if they'll learn to look for them. The goal, then, is to keep an eye out for needs that your students can do something about.

Role Play

To help your students practice seeing needs in others, have a few volunteers do the following role play. You will need a copy of the "Role Plays" worksheet, cut into four sections (one for each actor). Each actor will play the part of one of the people described on the worksheet. To ensure that they don't know each others' roles, give out the parts individually. (You can add other miscellaneous roles if you like.)

Explain that they each have a need that they have not shared with the others. True to human nature, they are all trying to keep their needs hidden (for whatever reason) from the others. Tell the actors to role play how their lunch conversation might go under these circumstances. Tell the audience to observe all the actors and try to discern each individual's need(s).

After two or three minutes, stop the action and ask the entire group (actors and audience) who has figured out what the individuals' needs are. If no one has, have the actors reveal their roles. Then resume the action, this time having the actors reveal their needs and having the others respond. Roll the action for another minute or two.

Afterward, thank the participants and discuss these two questions:

- **What makes it hard to see needs in others?** (Many times people try to hide their needs. We sometimes choose to ignore peoples' needs.
- **What makes it hard to do something about others' needs even if we've noticed them?** (We may be afraid of getting drawn into someone else's difficult problem; we may be afraid of being inconvenienced; we may feel like we're imposing on them if we acknowledge it or bring it up.)

Summarize by pointing out that helping others involves two steps: (1) seeing the needs, and (2) offering to help. Seeing needs in others takes *sensitivity*; offering to help takes *courage*.

CHALLENGE

(5 min.)

Discussion

Tell everyone to pause for a few moments to think of the times this past year when they needed help from someone but got none. Then ask: **What were your needs?** Take several answers. Explain that one of the best ways to become more sensitive to others' needs is to hear our friends tell about the times we overlooked their hurts.

Talk To

Then say something like: **Maybe all this talk of needs has made you think of someone you can help. I hope so. Jesus taught us to look out for others' needs with a clear picture of why it's important.**

Have a student read aloud Matthew 25:31-46.

Continue: **Watching for the needs of others and doing something about them is an important part of following Jesus. To see and act on those needs just takes a little practice.**

ACTION

(5 min.)

Prayer

Lead the students in a prayer, asking God to change their way of hearing and seeing people so that they can be more like Jesus.

While all eyes are closed, ask students to indicate by raising a hand if they have thought of someone they plan to help in some way over the next week. End the prayer time asking God to give students the opportunities and courage to do what they know they should do to help others.

Suggest that students talk to you if they are still unsure about what to do. You may be able to give them some ideas.

ACTIVE BONUS

"At Your Service"

Begin the meeting with this game. Divide into two teams and seat them in parallel columns at least eight feet away from the front of the room. Give each team a serving tray, and place a garbage bag filled with various items on the floor at the front of the room. Explain that at your signal, the first person from each team should come to the front, balancing the tray on one hand, pull an item out of the bag, place it on the tray, and carry it back to the next person on the team without dropping it. That person should repeat the process, adding another item to the tray.

If the tray falls or the items spill off, only the tray may be picked up from the floor, and the contest continues with new items being placed on the tray. After four minutes, the team with the most items on its tray wins.

Note: with a large and/or rowdy group, have separate bags of items to carry, one for each team.

Here are some items to include: a cotton ball, a paper cup, a rock or paperweight, a book, a spoon, a toothpick, a Ping-Pong ball, a pencil, a golf ball, a napkin, a salt shaker, and other unbreakable items of varying weights.

ADDITIONAL IDEA

"The Comfort Factor"

Have the group list the types of people that might cause some kids to be uncomfortable. The list could include: a loud person, a person always telling corny jokes, someone always telling dirty jokes, someone who swears a lot, a person of a different race, a person with a physical disability, someone very uncoordinated, a person with a mental disability, someone who usually smells bad, a person who always wears old or dirty clothes, a teacher's pet, etc.

Distribute pieces of paper and pencils or pens. Have students write the types of people down the left-hand side. Then, to the right, have them write the comfort factor for each: 1 = like being with this person; 2 = this person is OK; 3 = take this person as he/she comes; 4 = avoid this person; 5 = reject this person. Write this scale on the board so that they will know what numbers to use.

Afterward, total the numbers to see what kinds of people the group would tend to avoid or reject. Then discuss students' answers and how they really act toward those with whom they feel uncomfortable.

Role Plays

1. The setting is the school cafeteria, where you and your friends have come to eat lunch together, as you always do. You are all friends.

   You are having trouble with algebra. You need help from someone who knows the stuff and won't mind tutoring you, but you are too embarrassed to admit needing so much help, so you pretend everything is normal.

2. The setting is the school cafeteria, where you and your friends have come to eat lunch together, as you always do. You are all friends.

   You are supposed to have a student-parent-teacher conference in a few days, and you aren't sure what it's about or how it will go. You mainly need reassurance but you're too afraid to admit it, so you pretend everything is normal.

3. The setting is the school cafeteria, where you and your friends have come to eat lunch together, as you always do. You are all friends.

   You are depressed about your breakup with your boyfriend/girlfriend. You're not sure why; you just need someone to talk to. You are afraid of being branded as having psychological problems, so you pretend everything is normal.

4. The setting is the school cafeteria, where you and your friends have come to eat lunch together, as you always do. You are all friends.

   You need money for lunch. Everyone has sat down to eat, but you didn't bring a lunch and don't have any money. You're too embarrassed to ask, so you pretend everything is normal.

THREE

Have a Towel

KEY CONCEPT:	Selfless service
BIBLE PASSAGES:	John 13:1-17
OBJECTIVE:	As a result of this meeting, students will identify at least three actions similar to foot washing that they can take to serve others.
MATERIALS CHECKLIST:	☐ Bibles ☐ Pennies ☐ Large pan of warm, slightly soapy water ☐ Two towels ☐ Chalkboard and chalk or erasable-marker board and marker with the "Major Areas" chart already written on it ☐ Saltine crackers or apples
JUNIOR HIGH/MIDDLE SCHOOL ADAPTATION:	Because most early adolescents still think in concrete terms, the real-life illustration of foot-washing should make a dramatic impression. This lesson should work well—keep the Bible study moving and give specific suggestions for acts of selfless service that they can do.

Game: "Making Change"

Divide into at least three teams. Explain that you are going to have a contest involving loose change and that you will collect the change and give it to a good cause. Ask everyone to take out all the change that they will use in the game and are willing to donate. Bring a couple of dollars worth of pennies to distribute to those who have no change to give.

Explain that you will call out something that you need change for. The first team to get that amount of change together and send it to you with their team representative will win that round. They must leave the change with you and continue the competition with whatever change they have left. Play until most of the teams are out of money or until you run out of things to call for.

Call out the following amounts, preceding each with, "I need change for . . ."

- a nickel
- a quarter
- a toll (in Illinois, that's usually 40¢)
- a dollar
- a candy bar (check the price—usually 40-45 cents)
- the offering on Sunday (any amount is correct)
- a half dollar
- a bribe to the judge of this contest (award the round to the team giving you the most money)
- a dime
- penny loafers (two pennies)
- a penny

Object Lesson: "Foot-washing Demo"

This is not a skit, or even necessarily funny. Your students probably will not have seen an actual foot-washing. This requires the cooperation and preparation of a student. Not only should the student wear sandals or slippers to the meeting, but he or she should also make sure that his or her feet are dirty (as opposed to smelly). You will need a large pan of warm (not hot or cold) slightly soapy water and at least two towels. Have your materials out of sight and ask your student assistant not to explain to anyone who might notice why he or she isn't wearing shoes. (You may have a chance to remark later that several people noticed the lack of shoes and the dirty feet but either did nothing or poked fun at the person.)

After the opening game, "Making Change," tell the students that you will be giving a brief demonstration of the kind of attitude Jesus asked us to have as we move through the world. Ask for a volunteer. Choose your student assistant and have him or her take a seat in front.

Once the person is seated, say to the group: **Jesus asked us to treat others as we would want to be treated. It's what I would like us to learn. How could we treat** _____ (name of student) **in such** a way that we would be imitating and obeying Jesus? Someone may suggest washing the person's feet, but there may be other suggestions.

Then say that you'd like to show them what Jesus did in a similar situation (before you read about it). Bring out the towels and the pan of water, and wash the student's feet well. Be sure to replace the person's sandals or slippers rather than letting him or her do so.

Note that some kids may laugh or be embarrassed by this. Merely ignore this until you're done; then use the awkwardness to discuss why this scene made them feel that way.

STUDY
(15 min.)

Bible Study

Read and study this passage in three sections: A. John 13:1-5; B. John 13:6-11; C. John 13:12-17. Each time, read the verses aloud and then ask the questions listed below.

A. John 13:1-5
- **What do these verses say Jesus knew before He washed His disciples' feet?** (He knew that it was time for Him to leave the world; He knew that He had all things under His power and was returning to God.)
- **What did Jesus do as a result of what He knew?** (Verse 1—He showed them the full extent of His love; verse 3—He washed His disciples' feet.)

Point out that in Jesus' day, foot-washing before eating was like washing hands—almost a necessity in a hot and dusty part of the world where everyone wore sandals. But Jesus, as teacher, would have been the last one expected to do the foot-washing.

B. John 13:6-11
- **How did Jesus answer Peter's reluctance to let Jesus wash his feet?** (Verse 8—Jesus said that if He couldn't wash Peter's feet, Peter could have no part of Him.)
- **Jesus wanted to teach Peter a lesson about their relationship and about how to treat others. What did He want Peter to learn?** (Peter needed to submit to Christ to serve others.)

C. John 13:12-17
- **After Jesus washed the disciples' feet, what did He ask them?** (Verse 12—If they understood what He had done.)
- **What reason did Jesus give for His actions?** (He was giving the disciples an example to follow.)
- **What promise did Jesus give to those who follow His example?** (They would be blessed.)
- **What do you think the word "blessed" means?** (Rewarded by God.)

Ask what examples students can remember when people acted unselfishly toward them—like washing their feet. Give a personal example and encourage students to share.

Ask when they have been able to wash someone's feet by unexpectedly serving them.

CHALLENGE

(2 min.)

Say something like: **There is a real thrill about doing what isn't expected. To tell you the truth, most adults are surprised when a young person demonstrates real service. Almost anything you do in the way of helping others will be as unexpected as foot-washing. That's because many adults think young people are insensitive to the needs of others and only concerned about themselves. They would say that you expect others to do for you but you rarely do for others. You will demonstrate that you are growing up when you begin to see the needs of others and take steps to help them.**

ACTION

(5 min.)

Explain that there are three major areas in their lives right now: home, school, and church. Brainstorm for a few minutes some unexpected service actions that they personally could do in each of those areas. (For example, home: do chores that you aren't expected to do; school: hold someone's door; church: pick up used Communion cups without being asked.)

Write the three areas on the board and record their suggestions. After students have brainstormed, invite each person to choose at least one of the actions for each area and make an effort to carry it out during the following week. Make sure you take some time at the next meeting for review and feedback.

ACTIVE BONUS

"Kindly Words"

Begin the meeting with this game. It will help teach the point that service can be done in the way we speak to each other. Unexpectedly kind words wash over others and allow them to feel accepted.

This contest is similar to charades. Divide into two teams and have one team send a representative to the front of the room. Explain that you will give each competitor a phrase to communicate to the team. This is not charades, so they should not give hints with hand signals or body language. They must speak the phrase with the mouth closed. The team should listen carefully and guess what their person is saying. And they should keep guessing until they get it right or until time has expired. Alternate teams and keep track of their times (allow a maximum of 90 seconds for each phrase). The first time, have competitors speak with their mouths completely closed. For the second and third rounds, let them open their lips while keeping their teeth clenched together. The last two competitors should speak the phrase with their mouths full of saltine crackers or with apples clenched between their teeth.

Here are some phrases to use:

Round One
- I love you.
- You're great!

Round Two
- I really appreciate you.
- Thank you very much.

Round Three
- That was terrific!
- You are wonderful.

Round Four
- That was really a sweet thing to do.
- I don't know what I'd do without you.

ADDITIONAL IDEA

Service Day

Choose a Saturday when your group can donate their services to anyone in the church or community who needs their help. Work could include gardening, washing windows, cleaning, painting, or anything else your students can do. Be sure to do the work for free, with no strings attached. (If someone should try to compensate you for the work, politely refuse and explain that you are doing it out of a desire to serve. Don't mix service with other things!)

FOUR

Outward Bound!

KEY CONCEPT:	Taking Christ to the world
BIBLE PASSAGES:	Matthew 28:18-20; Acts 1:7-8
OBJECTIVE:	As a result of this meeting, students will be exposed to the basic questions that create a missionary view of life.
MATERIALS CHECKLIST:	☐ Bibles ☐ Pencils or pens ☐ Christian youth magazines ☐ Snacks that reflect foreign cuisine ☐ Copies of the "Global Quick Change" worksheet Active Bonus ☐ Old clothes
JUNIOR HIGH/MIDDLE SCHOOL ADAPTATION:	When using this lesson with junior highers, skip "Global Quick Change" and begin with "Language/Country Scavenger Hunt." During the Study, use fewer questions. And for Action, have students write their answers to each of the questions. Then help them design a specific plan of action.

STARTERS

(10 min.)

"Global Quick Change"

Hand out copies of the "Global Quick Change" worksheet and pencils or pens. Allow five minutes for students to match the two columns.

Here are the answers: 1. Berlin Wall; 2. Bill Clinton; 3. Baghdad, Iraq; 4. Soviet Union; 5. Somalia; 6. Tienanmen Square; 7. Hostages released; 8. Fidel Castro; 9. Boris Yeltsin; 10. Nelson Mandela; 11. Yugoslavia; 12. Haitians

"Language/Country Scavenger Hunt"

Divide into three groups. Ask each group to huddle with a secretary and see in how many different languages the group can say at least one word. They should write down the language and one representative word. They should also list the names of as many countries as possible.

After five minutes, have the groups report their lists of languages/words and countries. Award 25 points for each language represented by a unique word and 10 points for every country that only their group has listed. (For example, two teams can each get 25 points if one mentions "welkommen" and the other "ufda." But if they both mention "Norway" as a country, neither gets the points.) Give the Global Consciousness Award to the winning team by allowing them to go last to the refreshments, or by having them serve refreshments to the rest of the group.

STUDY

(20 min.)

Bible Study

Have a student read Matthew 28:18-20 aloud. Have another student read Acts 1:7-8 aloud. Then discuss:

- **What did Jesus tell the disciples to do?** (To go into all the world, making disciples, and baptizing in His name.)
- **Where did Jesus send the disciples?** (Into all the world, beginning with Jerusalem, Judea, and Samaria, and then to the ends of the earth.)
- **What time and location limits did Jesus mention?** (Until the end of the age and to the ends of the world.)
- **Where were the disciples supposed to start?** (At home—in Jerusalem, Judea, and Samaria.)
- **What would be the keys to their effectiveness?** (The Holy Spirit would give them power.)
- **If you had been present at either of these occasions, what would have been your plan of action?**
- **Why is it important for at least some Christians to go to the "ends of the world"** (that is, to other nations)?
- **What can Christians do who for some reason can't go?** (Go to the people near them, and support those who can go elsewhere.)

CHALLENGE

(10 min.)

Discussion

Say something like: **The biggest obstacles to following Christ are the questions that we have. But God's answers rarely come until we are committed to being guided by Him. In other words, we must be willing to do what God wants before we will begin to see His answers.**

Place the following three questions each in its own separate envelope, have your group divide into three smaller groups, and have each group take one of the envelopes. Ask them to spend three minutes discussing their answer to the question they find inside.

Here are the questions:

1. What do you consider most challenging about the idea of going to another country as a missionary?
2. What are some of the ways you are able to share your faith with others?
3. How can you serve God right where you are?

Encourage the groups to discuss these questions by having everyone give his or her own answer to the question.

After three minutes, ask the groups to share their answers. Invite everyone to answer, but don't force anybody. Also, ask in the order the questions are listed. Let this time of sharing be an opportunity for them to challenge each other.

ACTION

(5 min.)

Pray

Lead the group in silent prayer, rephrasing the questions from "Challenge": What is challenging to me about being a missionary? How can I share my faith with others? How can I serve God better right where I am? Repeat the questions, one at a time, allowing time for students to talk to God about them.

ACTIVE BONUS

"Short Term Mission"

This could replace the Starters. This will require preparation, but it should be well worth the added effort.

Have students meet at an appointed place that can also be their last stop of the night. In between, they will travel to at least four other locations as follows.

1. WARDROBE: An ideal setting would be the garage of someone who has just had a large garage sale and wouldn't mind you raiding the leftovers before taking them to a charity. Tell students to look through the assortment of clothes and find new outfits to wear on their

mission experience. Except for underwear, they should completely change the rest of their clothes and shoes. Provide separate areas for girls and guys to change and give them plastic bags in which to carry their "old clothes."

2. TRAINING—Packing for the Mission Field: Organize the group into one large circle or smaller circles of 10 to 15 each. Explain that part of their preparation will involve packing. Designate a person in each circle to begin and explain that they should move clockwise around the circle. The first person should say, "I went to the mission field and I took with me _____" (something needed on the field: for example, "Proof that I had taken all the required shots!"). The next person should repeat the sentence, saying what the first person did and adding his or her own item. Continue until they go completely around the circle. For a twist, you could change the sentence in the middle to: "When I got to the mission field, I discovered that I really didn't need my _____."

3. TRAINING—Language: At this point, explain that they will have to use a new language in the missions experience. Have students number off by threes. Explain that they must now use the word "blank" in place of every first, second, or third word they say depending on the number they got when everyone counted off by threes. Use the sentence, "This will be a very interesting experience" to illustrate what they must do:

a. "Blank will be blank very interesting blank."
b. "This blank be a blank interesting experience."
c. "This will blank a very blank experience."

4. SERVICE: Next, students should be transported to a place where they can be involved in some effort of service. Depending on the group, consider doing something that might cause a little embarrassment, such as cleaning up the local park or caroling out of season at the home of a shut-in. Even a walk through a local mall where they straighten chairs at the eating area might be interesting to the group. It would certainly cause a stir.

5. DEBRIEF: This part can take several directions. You might ask them to reflect on their brief experiences of the evening, comparing what they felt and saw with what a missionary might experience going into a foreign culture. If you can arrange for a missionary to speak to the group, try to make sure that he or she hears this discussion. It will uncover some of the stereotypes that students have of missionary life and work. Then that person can address those ideas in his or her talk. It would be helpful to arrange for such a speaker to interact with the students afterward.

6. FOOD: Transport the students back to the starting point for refreshments. Be sure to arrange for a variety of foreign dishes and treats.

Global Quick Change

Match the Quick Change places and events on the left with the names and descriptions on the right.

1. Not Humpty, but it came tumbling down   a. Baghdad, Iraq

2. Arkansas winner   b. Somalia

3. Scud city   c. Hostages released

4. Coup, recovery, collapse   d. Tienanmen Square

5. Famine and civil war   e. Boris Yeltsin

6. A democratic party at the quadrilateral park   f. Bill Clinton

7. Home at last!   g. Soviet Union

8. Last lonely Communist big shot   h. Yugoslavia

9. "Georgia on my mind!"   i. Nelson Mandela

10. South Africa   j. Haitians

11. Former nation of Bosnians   k. Fidel Castro

12. Flooding to U.S. in boats   l. Berlin Wall

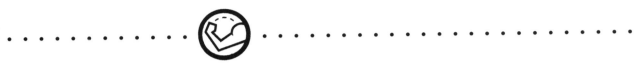

STEWARDSHIP

FIVE

You Gotta Get These Gifts

KEY CONCEPT:	Using spiritual gifts
BIBLE PASSAGES:	1 Corinthians 12–14 and other selected passages
OBJECTIVE:	As a result of this meeting, students will understand the importance of using their gifts to serve the body of Christ.
MATERIALS CHECKLIST:	☐ Bibles ☐ Pencils or pens ☐ Balloons ☐ Buckets ☐ Prizes (candy) ☐ Chalkboard and chalk or erasable-marker board and marker ☐ Butcher paper ☐ Toilet paper ☐ Envelopes with instructions inside ☐ Copies of the "Spiritual Gifts Worksheet"
JUNIOR HIGH/MIDDLE SCHOOL ADAPTATION:	Junior highers should know about spiritual gifts, but this lesson could be too conceptual if you're not careful. Keep it moving, and use concrete illustrations of the gifts. Also, assign adult leaders for the small groups. Then, for Action, discuss specific ways for kids to become involved in church.

STARTER

(10 min.)

"Got Something For You!"

Choose couples to compete. These may be pairs of friends or team representatives. Give each couple a bucket and a balloon. Explain that the goal of this game is to see how many times a team can catch the balloon in its bucket in two minutes.

Here's how it works. A person from each couple stands at one end of the room. This person is the catcher and he or she holds the bucket. As a balloon approaches, the catcher may reach, bend at the waist, etc. but is not permitted to move his or her feet and must always keep both hands on the bucket. The other person from each couple should stand about ten feet away, behind a starting line.

The batter should have a balloon which, at the signal, he or she should bat toward the bucket. The balloon may only be batted with the hands — it may not be picked up or held.

After a couple's balloon has been batted to the catcher and caught in the bucket, the catcher and batter should change positions and roles (in other words, the catcher should become the batter and vice versa). The process should continue until time has expired. The couple catching the balloon the most times wins.

Note: Be sure to assign someone to each couple to count their catches.

As a transition, point out that this is a simple illustration of how spiritual gifts work: they involve people working together.

STUDY

(20 min.)

Bible Study

Introduce the Bible study by explaining that Scripture is filled with lists and descriptions of spiritual gifts. Before looking at these lists, give this simple definition of spiritual gift: A spiritual gift is an ability for service that God gives to a Christian.

Explain that this definition highlights two facts:

1. Spiritual gifts are special abilities given by God—not just natural talents.
2. Spiritual gifts are given by God so that Christians might serve one another, and not just themselves.

Distribute pencils or pens and copies of the "Spiritual Gifts Worksheet." Divide the group into four smaller groups and assign each a different passage from the Worksheet (1 Corinthians 12:4-11; Romans 12:3-8; Ephesians 4:7, 11-13; or 1 Peter 4:8-11). Explain that each group should list all the gifts mentioned in their passage.

After they finish, get everyone's attention and have the groups share their findings. Combine all their lists on the board. Here's a compilation of what they will probably mention:

- prophecy
- pastor
- teaching
- wisdom
- knowledge
- exhortation
- giving
- helps
- mercy
- missionary
- evangelism
- hospitality
- faith
- leadership
- administration
- miracles
- healing
- tongues
- interpretation
- intercession
- service

Rather than defining each and every gift, ask your students if any of these need clarification. Define or discuss only those that they mention. (For a more complete or exhaustive set of definitions, ask your pastor for references or see C. Peter Wagner's book, *Your Spiritual Gifts Can Help Your Church Grow* [Glendale, Calif., Regal Books, 1974].)

Discussion

Once you've got your list, discuss the following questions briefly:

- **Who are the most gifted people in our church?**
- **Who are the most spiritual people in our church?**

Take several answers to both questions, and be sure to ask what makes those people gifted or spiritual.

Have a student read 1 Corinthians 12:1 aloud. **Ask: Why do you think God wants us to know about spiritual gifts?** (So we can use them properly.)

Discuss:

- **If a soccer team shows up with just nine players to play against a team with all eleven positions filled, what will happen?** (The team with fewer players will probably lose.)
- **If someone in a church has the gift of teaching and doesn't use it, what will be the effect on everyone else?** (Many people will not learn.)

Say something like: **The bottom line is this: If we don't use our spiritual gifts, *everyone* loses out—we don't benefit from those gifts, other people don't benefit from those gifts, and everyone has to make up for what isn't done.**

But in order to use our gifts, we must know what they are. So we must search the Scriptures and ask God to show us our spiritual gifts. Then we should experiment in various kinds of service.

Now have the groups take a few minutes to discuss and write down ways a Christian can use each of the gifts they listed. Afterward, ask them to share what they wrote. (Have a list of the gifts and their definitions handy.) Here are some suggestions:

Teaching	start a Bible study teach in Vacation Bible School or Sunday School
Knowledge	help plan events and programs
Exhortation	counsel hurting friends
Giving	give to the church
Helps	help in any area of the church you would enjoy
Mercy	volunteer as a candystriper go on a mission trip
Evangelism	share the Gospel weekly
Hospitality	greet new people at church or youth group
Faith	start a prayer chain
Leadership	offer to lead youth group meetings set the example when at church activities
Administration	keep group records set up meeting agendas
Service	go on a mission trip help clean up after meetings

Note: This list is not exhaustive; it's merely a place to start. Some of these gifts may not apply directly to your students at this time in their lives, but then again you (or they) may think of ways that they do. Feel free to add to this list any suggestions you have.

CHALLENGE

(5 min.)

Talk To

Remind everyone that identifying our spiritual gifts and using them properly is necessary for the Church to be what God wants it to be. We must obey God's command to know and use our spiritual gifts to make His Body work in this world the way He designed it to work.

To close, read 1 Corinthians 13:1-8 aloud while everyone follows along—a reminder of the need for love in the use of spiritual gifts. Mention that this famous "love chapter" was written to place balance in our use of our gifts.

ACTION

(10 min.)

Response

Have each person share what he or she believes his or her spiritual gift(s) to be. Have the group suggest to each person what his or her spiritual gifts might be. Have students respond with specific places or applications for using their gifts this week.

ACTIVE BONUS

"Gift Wrap"

Bring a number of odd-shaped items such as: a football, a necklace, pliers, a water balloon, a coat hanger, a small pillow, etc., but keep them out of sight for now. Have volunteers come to the front. Give them wrapping paper and tape and have them stand behind a table. Explain that this will be a contest to see who can do the best job of wrapping an item in two minutes. Then bring out blindfolds and put them on the competitors. Place an item to wrap in front of each competitor and give the signal to start.

ADDITIONAL IDEAS

"Down in Arms"

Have the entire group stand in a circle with everyone locking arms with the kids on both sides of them. On a given signal have everyone sit down while keeping their arms locked. Then with arms still joined, have everyone stand again. Use this as a general illustration of teamwork.

"Gifted Ones"

Discuss individuals in your church whose spiritual gifts are obvious. Ask how your students knew about the gifts and how the gifts are being used in church.

Spiritual Gifts Worksheet

HOW I CAN FUNCTION IN THE BODY OF CHRIST

The Gifts   **How I Can Use Them**

- 1 Corinthians 12:4-11

- Romans 12:3-8

- Ephesians 4:7, 11-13

- 1 Peter 4:8-11

SIX

Put Your Best Foot Forward

KEY CONCEPT:	Using personal abilities and talents to help others and glorify God
BIBLE PASSAGES:	Matthew 25:31-46; 2 Corinthians 5:15; 1 Peter 4:10-11
OBJECTIVE:	As a result of this meeting, students will be able to identify a personal ability or talent and how it can be used to glorify God.
MATERIALS CHECKLIST:	☐ Bibles ☐ Pencils or pens ☐ 4" X 6" index cards ☐ Matthew 25 posterboard ☐ "Under-Valued Talents" poster or chalkboard ☐ Copies of the "Talent Scout" worksheet
JUNIOR HIGH/MIDDLE SCHOOL ADAPTATION:	This can be a very helpful and practical lesson for junior highers because they have the need to feel competent. Identifying special talents and abilities can be a very positive and confidence-building experience. The lesson should work well as written; just keep the Study moving so that it doesn't become a lecture. If kids don't offer suggestions for the categories on the board, give examples of skills and talents and have kids put them in the appropriate categories.

STARTER
(10 min.)

"Star Search"

Hand out copies of the "Talent Scout" worksheets. Tell students to move around the room and act as talent scouts, finding people to fit each category. They should get a signature for each line.

After a few minutes stop and see who has the most signatures. Then have a number of volunteers display their weird talents for the rest of the group.

STUDY
(20 min.)

List

Introduce the study by saying something like: **Our topic is: How to use talents and abilities to serve God. Some of you may think you don't *have* any talents or abilities. So we'll start right there!**

Every person is talented because every person has been created that way by God. Do you believe it? You may have labeled yourself a non-talented, low ability person because you don't have an outstanding performance skill such as playing a sport or a musical instrument, singing, or acting in drama or comedy. Our society loves people with those abilities and pays them a lot of money. But that makes the rest of us feel as though we have no talents. We do.

Invite your students to make a list of undervalued talents—the special skills people rely on when they need something done for them. Write these four categories on the board: technical skills, practical skills, artistic skills, character skills. Have everyone call out suggestions as you write them on the board under the appropriate categories. Here are some examples:

Technical	Practical	Artistic	Character or Personal
Electrical Repair	Cooking/feeding	Writing	Listening
Machine Repair	Organizing	Song Writing	Counseling
Computer Programming	Child Care	Poetry	Hospitality
Car Repair	Teaching	Painting	Generosity
Typing Keyboarding	Individual Sports	Photography	Encouragement
Carpentry	Yard Work	Drawing	Friendship, Building up Others

After completing your list, continue: **I'm sure that there are more than we can list. Can you see some special skills or abilities that people in our group possess? How about yourself?** Take a few answers.

Small Groups

Next, break into small groups—encourage students to gather with others who know them well. Distribute 4" X 6" index cards and pencils or pens.

Tell everyone to write their names at the top. Then have them pass their cards to the right. Each person should write a sincere comment suggesting the abilities and talents they see in the person (either presently or potentially) whose name is on the card.

Pass the cards again after about a minute. Continue until everyone in the small group has written on every card. Then, one at a time, have kids read aloud what is written about the person on the card they are holding. After each card is read, it should be returned to its owner.

Caution: Alert volunteers and student leaders to scatter themselves evenly into all groups and to give special attention to any cards where not much has been written.

Afterward, bring everyone back together and focus on the list of undervalued talents. Read off each talent, one at a time, and ask students to stand who have that talent or skill written on their cards. See how many talents are represented in your group.

CHALLENGE

(5 min.)

Discussion

Say something like: **Let's be honest—many of us would like our talents to propel us to fame and stardom. We'd like to be so good at what we do that we get paid tons of money and receive lots of fan mail for our genius. Though that may happen, I urge you to consider a better goal for your God-given skills.**

Have a student read 2 Corinthians 5:15 aloud. (Have it read in several different translations if possible.) It says that Christians ''. . . should no longer live for themselves but for Him who died for them and was raised again.'' After reading it, ask:

- **What does 2 Corinthians 5:15 tell us about our talents?** (We should use them to serve God.)
- **What difference does it make for people using the talents on our list?** Direct everyone's attention to the list of talents and abilities. That is, have them describe the difference between an ability used for oneself and one used for God. How would a person do yard work if he or she were serving God in the process? if he or she were serving him or herself? Have your students describe the difference for several of these talents.
- **How will we be judged for using our talents and abilities? Look at Matthew 25:31-46.** Have one of the students read the passage aloud. Note that there is no mention of fame or fortune—just service: feeding people, housing people, clothing people, visiting people, and caring for people.

To sum up: We have talents and abilities so we can serve one another, not so we can awe the world with our greatness.

Self-evaluation

Say something like: **Look at your** (4" X 6" index) **card—you each have talents and abilities. The important question is: How are you using your talents and abilities? If you can repair cars, cook food, write letters, or do dirty work, God can use you to help others. Your life will count for something that will *last* forever.**

So here's my challenge: Have a student read 1 Peter 4:10-11 aloud: "God has given each of you special abilities; be sure to use them to help each other, passing on to others God's many kinds of blessings. Are you called to preach? Then preach as though God Himself were speaking through you. Are you called to help others? Do it with all the strength and energy that God supplies, so that He will be glorified through Jesus Christ—to Him be glory and power forever and ever. Amen" (TLB).

ACTION

(10 min.)

Analysis

Have students look again at their talents/abilities card. Tell them to write the name of someone they can help next to each one of their talents and abilities. If they don't know an individual who fits, they should write a group or place where they can contribute.

Then, pray together and ask God to use them and yourself to serve others and glorify Him.

ACTIVE BONUS

"Relay Talented"

Play this game at the beginning of the meeting, before "Star Search."

Divide into teams and give each one an envelope with a set of talents written on slips of paper. Explain that at your signal the first person should draw out a slip of paper, run to the front of the room, and perform the talent. The first team to finish all the talents wins. Talents to write on the slips of paper could include: Write and read aloud a six line poem; act out an argument between a parent and teenager over curfew (both parts); beat out eight measures of 4/4 time; make five people smile, etc.

ADDITIONAL IDEA

Put together a youth group "Talent Resource Directory" in which you list each group member and his or her talents.

Talent Scout

TALENTS ONLY A MOTHER WOULD BE PROUD OF

See if you can find people (or other life forms) with each of the talents listed below. See if you can get someone to sign his or her name, paw print, or patent number to each one.

1. Can make a bizarre face

2. Can make a strange sound with his or her lips

3. Can do strange tricks with his or her tongue

4. Can do an impression of an animal

5. Can do a weird body movement

6. Can make a strange hand movement

7. Can contort his or her body parts

8. Can do something strange with his or her toes

9. Can display an unusual speech pattern

10. Free choice—weird talent: _____

SEVEN

Opportunity Knocks

KEY CONCEPT:	Managing God's gifts to us
BIBLE PASSAGES:	Selected passages
OBJECTIVE:	As a result of this meeting, students will learn about the opportunities God gives them to further His kingdom.
MATERIALS CHECKLIST:	☐ Bibles ☐ Pencils or pens ☐ Index cards ☐ Scratch paper ☐ Copies of the "Opportunity Knocks" worksheet ☐ Copies of the "Carpe Diem Manifesto" worksheet
JUNIOR HIGH/MIDDLE SCHOOL ADAPTATION:	This lesson should work well with junior highers if it is simplified and made very concrete. Begin with the Active Bonus game, "Red Light, Green Light" instead of "I Regret" or "Life Goals." When filling out the "Opportunity Knocks" worksheets, divide into small groups, each led by an adult. Do the same with "Carpe Diem Manifesto."

STARTERS
(10 min.)

"I Regret"

Hand out index cards and pencils or pens. Tell students to write their anonymous responses to two or three of the following questions:

- I really regret . . .
- If only I had . . .
- If I could relive last month, the things I would do differently are . . .
- If I knew that I was going to die today, I would be sad that I never . . .

Collect the cards and read some of the responses aloud.

"Life Goals"

Hand out scratch paper and have students come up with a list of 25 wild things they would like to do or accomplish before they die. Tell them to dream big or to think in terms of being 80 years old and looking back on their lives, having lived in such a way that they have no regrets at all!

After everyone has a long list, ask several volunteers to share some of the opportunities and goals on their lists.

STUDY
(20 min.)

"Opportunity Knocks"

Distribute copies of the "Opportunity Knocks" worksheet. Explain that this sheet lists five general commands that God gives all Christians—to learn (about God and the Christian life), to share the Gospel, to grow in Christ, to help others, and to learn and follow God's will. These commands represent *opportunities* God gives us to further His kingdom; when we obey Him in these ways, we further His kingdom.

Tell students to choose one of the categories that they would like to investigate. They can read the Scriptures and circle the ones that fit their kind of opportunity. Then they should describe how God wants us to seize that opportunity—what students can do to further God's kingdom.

Have them fill these out individually, on their own.

(Note: Unless you have a group of 15 or more students, don't worry if one of the categories goes unchosen. You want them to look into issues that interest them.)

Discussion

After everyone has worked on this exercise silently for about five minutes, discuss what they found. Here are the opportunities and suggestions for each one:

The Opportunity	How to Seize It
1. To Learn about God and the Christian Life	Hebrews 10:24-25—go to church, Bible study, youth group meetings, or

The Opportunity (cont.)	How to Seize It (cont.)
	other gatherings of Christians 1 Timothy 4:7 — avoid superstitions; train yourself
2. To Share the Gospel	Colossians 4:5 — whenever you are around non-Christians, act in a way that shows them Christ Romans 1:13-16 — do not be ashamed to tell others about Christ Ephesians 5:15-16 — make the most of every opportunity
3. To Grow	Hebrews 10:24-25 — whenever you meet with other Christians, learn from them 1 Peter 2:2 — crave every chance to learn
4. To Help Others	Hebrews 3:13 — encourage each other Galatians 6:1-2, 10 — bear others' burdens; do good to others Hebrews 10:24-25 — encourage others to love and obey God 1 Thessalonians 5:14 — urge others to follow Jesus; encourage them
5. To Find Out and Follow God's Will	Romans 12:1-2 — conform your thinking to God's perspective Hebrews 10:24-25 — learn from others at church

Here are some questions to use:

- **Why do we miss out (or choose to miss out) on so many good opportunities to advance the work of God in the world?** (Often we get distracted or forget about God's priorities.)
- **What happens when we pass up an opportunity that God drops in our laps?**
- **What are some examples of the kinds of opportunities listed above?** Tell them to think of specific opportunities God has given them in each of the five areas.

CHALLENGE

(5 min.)

Talk To

Say something like: **Every day God drops into our lives dozens of opportunities for serving Him. There are lessons we can learn if we'll take the** time; people who need help and who are hurting; friends who would be willing to listen to the Gospel; and many other opportunities to exercise our faith.

But many of these lessons and situations are once-in-a-lifetime. So if we pass them up or fail to take advantage of them, we miss out. And in many cases others miss out too. They don't get helped, or told, or encouraged.

Life's too short to miss these prime opportunities. Let's look for chances to learn, grow, and serve; otherwise, we'll one day look back and have regrets.

ACTION
(10 min.)

"Carpe Diem Manifesto"

Have students write out a "plan of attack" for the next seven days using the "Carpe Diem Manifesto" worksheet. Give students about three minutes to fill them out; then have them share their plans. Finally, have everyone get signatures from their accountability partners (make sure everyone has one).

Close with prayers of commitment, asking God to make us better stewards of His resources.

ACTIVE BONUS

"Red Light, Green Light"

This children's game illustrates the importance of seizing the opportunity. One student is "it." He or she should stand at one end of the room or field facing the rest of the group, which is located at the other end of the room or field. As "it" turns his or her back to the group, he or she says "green light." This gives everyone the opportunity to run forward. But at any moment, "it" can yell "red light," and then spin back around and face the group. If he or she sees people still moving, those caught must return to the starting line. The first one to touch "it" gets to be "it" the next time.

ADDITIONAL IDEAS

Video

Show the scene(s) from the movie, "Dead Poet's Society," in which the teacher (played by Robin Williams) urges his students to "seize the day," and "to suck the marrow out of life." Discuss what this means for a Christian. You can use Video Movies Worth Watching (Dave Veerman, editor, Baker Book House, 1992) for more details on how to incorporate this idea into a meeting.

Opportunity Knocks

Choose an area of opportunity from the five possibilities listed. Then circle the Scripture passages that tell us how to seize that opportunity for God and His kingdom. (You may find more than one passage that fits.) Then describe in your own words how to seize that opportunity!

Opportunities God Gives Us

1. To Learn about God and the Christian life
How to seize the opportunity:

2. To share the Gospel
How to seize the opportunity:

3. To grow in Christ
How to seize the opportunity:

4. To help Others
How to seize the opportunity:

5. To find out and follow God's will
How God wants us to seize the opportunity:

Scriptures that apply to opportunity number _____ (circle all that apply):

Romans 1:13-16	Romans 12:1-2	1 Timothy 4:7
1 Thessalonians 5:14	Galatians 6:1-2, 10	Ephesians 5:15-16
Colossians 4:5	Hebrews 3:13	Hebrews 10:24-25
		1 Peter 2:2

Carpe Diem Manifesto

I will "seize the day" each day next week by:

_____

_____

_____

_____

_____

_____

I will specifically take advantage of these opportunities

to learn:	to share my faith:	to grow:	to help others:
_____	_____	_____	_____
_____	_____	_____	_____
_____	_____	_____	_____
_____	_____	_____	_____
_____	_____	_____	_____
_____	_____	_____	_____
_____	_____	_____	_____

I will ask _____ to pray for me and to ask me how I am doing in my quest to become a better manager of the opportunities God gives me.

Signed _____

Witness/Accountability Partner _____ Date _____

EIGHT

Charles Schlob—Not

KEY CONCEPT:	Investing gifts, talents, and abilities wisely
BIBLE PASSAGE:	Matthew 25:14-30
OBJECTIVE:	As a result of this meeting, students will learn how to invest, rather than just use, their talents and abilities.
MATERIALS CHECKLIST:	☐ Bibles ☐ Pencils or pens ☐ Copies of the investment section of the newspaper (with a key to the codes) ☐ Copies of the "Mutual Life Examiners" worksheet ☐ Copies of the "Life Investment" worksheet
JUNIOR HIGH/MIDDLE SCHOOL ADAPTATION:	Because this is the last lesson in the series on Stewardship, it will be a good review and reinforcement of the truth that God has given all Christians abilities, talents, and spiritual gifts to invest for His kingdom. For junior highers, "Carry or Bury" (Active Bonus) will work better than "Investment Dot-to-dot." Use the "Mutual Life Examiners" worksheet, but lead students through the process from the front. Don't use the "Life Investment" worksheet with this age group. Instead, discuss this with the whole group.

STARTERS
(10 min.)

"Investment Dot-to-dot"

Beforehand photocopy a page out of the investment section of your local newspaper. Hand out copies and pencils or pens, and give a coded list of directions for drawing dots on the page. Explain that when the dots are connected, they will form a familiar picture (a big dollar sign). The code should be something students can find on the page (like the increase in a certain stock). They should put dots in the right spots (according to the codes) and then connect the dots. You should have three chains of codes: one for the S-shape and one each for each of the two vertical slashes.

Give a dollar to the first student who puts the marks on the sheet, connects the dots, and brings you the dollar sign. (To be fair, check to be sure all the dots are connected.)

"Mutual Life Examiners" worksheet

Distribute the "Mutual Life Examiners" worksheets. Have everyone fill out the worksheets, analyzing their current personal investments. After a few minutes, have volunteers share their numbers.

STUDY
(23 min.)

Drama

Have your students break into groups of four to five. Tell them to read Matthew 25:14-30 (the parable of the talents) and come up with a short drama depicting the passage in a contemporary setting. Allow about five to seven minutes for preparation; then have each small group perform for everyone else.

Discussion

Afterward, discuss these questions:

- **What does "investment" mean?** (Doing something small for the purpose of getting something larger or more valuable in return.)
- **How do you choose where to invest your time and energy?**
- **Every investment involves risk. Is it better to take that risk or to play it safe and not invest at all? Why?** Normally, responses would probably differ from student to student. But after reading the parable, they will more likely say that it's better to take the risk if God is behind your efforts.
- **How can someone invest a skill?** (Train, practice, learn from others.)
- **How important are the people around you in how you invest your talents and gifts?** See what students say. Most will probably recognize that the people around them can play an important role in their lives.
- **What role does God play in our investment of talents and gifts?** (He causes us to grow when we invest them in His kingdom.)

Explain that the passage just read indicates that in God's economy investment is not a choice—wise investment in the things of God is a *must*. The bottom line of this parable is: "Use it or lose it."

Then ask:

- **What things do you have to invest in the Kingdom of God?**
- **How could you invest these resources more effectively?**

CHALLENGE
(2 min.)

Talk To

Say something like: **The challenge for us is to recognize the gifts, abilities, and talents that God has given us and invest them wisely. Sometimes this can be difficult because the world's values often differ from God's. The challenge for us is not to be selfish (like the third servant in the parable) and bury what gifts God has given us, but to invest our resources on our Master's behalf.**

ACTION
(12 min.)

"Life Investment"

Pass out copies of the "Life Investment" worksheet. Tell everyone to start on the far right, coming up with a goal for their lives. This may be very difficult for students, so circulate throughout the group and help them. Some students may write: "To play a professional sport." Others may write: "To become a doctor." Still others may say: "To glorify God." After everyone has written a life goal, have them use Column 1 to list one to five gifts, abilities, and talents they have that could help them meet that goal. Then have them fill in Columns 2, 3, and 4 for each gift, ability, or talent.

Ask how they have been investing for their goal and to share a few ideas for investing.

Have the group take a moment to reflect on what gifts, talents, and abilities they have as a group. Discuss ways to use these gifts, talents, and abilities in your church. Make specific plans for using some of them during the next few weeks. Check on each other's results at the next group meeting.

Close by having kids pray for each other to be wise investors during the coming week.

ACTIVE BONUS

"Carry or Bury"

Divide into teams and give each team a stack of scratch paper and pencils. Tell them to write one talent on each sheet of paper. These talents should be real and should be possessed by team members. Also, there should be no repetition. Then have the teams crumple the scratch paper into individual balls and put them in a pile at the front of the team. Line up the teams in parallel columns behind their talents at least 10 feet from the front of the room.

Explain that this will be a race to see which team can carry the most talents at one time, within one minute. At your signal the first person should take one talent and carry it to the front of the room and back to his or her team and hand it to the next team member, who should add a talent and run to the front and back. Each person should add a talent. The team holding the most talents at the end of the time wins. Read their talents aloud.

ADDITIONAL IDEA

Video

A copy of the film, ''One in a Million'' (Mars Hill Productions) would help to illustrate the point made about the world's values differing from God's.

Mutual Life Examiners

The Investment Portfolio of: _____

Time: List the number of hours per week you invest in the following areas (maximum 168):

_____ Close friends   _____ Sports   _____ Home life   _____ God

_____ Family   _____ School   _____ Hobbies   _____ Talent

_____ Acquaintances   _____ Job   _____ Personal time   _____ Other

Money: List the approximate number of dollars you invest per week on the following:

_____ Food   _____ Entertainment   _____ Transportation   _____ Savings

_____ Clothes   _____ School   _____ Charity   _____ Other

Thought: List the approximate number of hours per week you invest in thinking about the following areas (168 maximum):

_____ Family   _____ Self-faults   _____ Self-strengths   _____ Future

_____ School   _____ God   _____ Opposite sex   _____ Past subjects

_____ Dreams   _____ Sports   _____ Relationship   _____ Other

Life Investment

1	2	3	4	5
My Gifts, Abilities, & Talents	How I've Used Them in the Past	How I Could Use Them Now	How I Might Use Them 10 Years from Now	My Life Goal

STRESS

NINE

Schedule Me Beautiful

KEY CONCEPT:	Managing stress from busy schedules
BIBLE PASSAGES:	Selected passages
OBJECTIVE:	As a result of this meeting, students experiencing stress will know how to analyze their schedules and make changes to reduce stress.
MATERIALS CHECKLIST:	☐ Bibles ☐ Pencils or pens ☐ Balloons ☐ Printed character descriptions or students prepared to present them ☐ Poster of Stress Characteristics ☐ Copies of the ''You Make the Call'' worksheet ☐ Copies of the ''Where Does All the Time Go?'' worksheet Active Bonus ☐ Blindfolds ☐ Shaving cream ☐ Straight razors
JUNIOR HIGH/MIDDLE SCHOOL ADAPTATION:	This is an important topic for junior highers because often they want to do every activity offered and can become too busy and stressed out. The Starters should work well. Use the ''Where Does All the Time Go?'' worksheet and use volunteers to act out the ''You Make the Call'' characters. Go through the ''Less Stress Normula Formulas'' worksheet together, but don't go through the ''Application Discussion'' in Challenge. Instead, explain two or three steps that kids can take to organize their time better.

STARTER
(8 min.)

"Stranger Arranger"

Divide the group into small groups of five to ten. When you give the desired order, they should see which team can place themselves in that order first:

- oldest to youngest with youngest in front
- by months of their birthdays with January in front
- alphabetical order by first name; Z in front
- by number of siblings; largest number in front
- by height with the shortest in front

For variation, blindfold the students, or require silence during the game.

STUDY
(25 min.)

Time Worksheet

Pass out the "Where Does All the Time Go?" worksheets and pencils or pens. Have students fill out the worksheets, marking their use of hours during a typical week. Allow 10 minutes for this.

Discussion

Afterward, have a three- to five-minute discussion using the following questions:

- **What takes up most of your time?**
- **What in your schedule causes you the most stress?**
- **What do you wish you had more time to do?**
- **How do you think God would want you to adjust or change your use of time?**

After three to five minutes of discussion, move on to the following activity.

Dramatizations

Cut the "You Make the Call" worksheet into three pieces and recruit three students to role play the characters described (Tina Overload, Bobby Brainstorm, and Donny Disaster), one actor for each character. (If you don't have enough students to do a dramatization, have everyone read the descriptions and discuss them one at a time.) Divide the rest of the class into small groups of four to five students each. Have the first actor read (dramatically) Tina Overload's monologue. Then have everyone else play counselor, discussing among themselves what advice they would give Tina on how to handle the stress in her life. After five minutes of small group discussion, have the small groups share their advice with the whole group. Then move on to the next dramatization, and repeat the process.

Discussion

After all three dramatizations, ask: **How can you tell if the stress levels in your life are too high?** Discuss briefly. Then explain that stress is too high if they are experiencing several of the following symptoms (write these on a posterboard or overhead transparency and display at the appropriate time):

- nervousness
- frequent crying
- irritability
- difficulty sleeping
- loss of appetite
- inability to concentrate

- depression
- fatigue
- headaches
- binge eating
- skin problems
- general apathy

CHALLENGE

(7 min.)

Application Discussion

Reassemble everyone into a large group. Write the following five main points on the board and simply ask what your students think each means. Discuss how these statements can help us reduce stress. Spend no more than seven minutes on this activity.

Use the bullet lists and other explanatory information that follows to help you prepare for the discussion; don't summarize it for your students.

1. STOP *killing or wasting time*

- We shouldn't get so preoccupied with what is not yet and, in fact, may never be (future hopes) that we miss out on what actually is (present reality).
- We shouldn't view our days and hours (perhaps even years) as a means to an end.
- We shouldn't squander our time on activities that are worthless and meaningless. Instead, we should choose the best right now.
- See Ephesians 5:15-16.

2. STOP *trying to turn back time*

- We can't undo past actions. We can't go back in time and do things over. We need to realize that:

  a. Today's choices produce tomorrow's consequences.
  b. Today's opportunities may not be around tomorrow. (See Numbers 14:40-45.)

3. START *understanding time*

- Our time on earth is fading quickly. In a blur, or in a blink, this life will be over. Every time the clock ticks, it brings us one second closer to the end.
- We need to develop an eternal perspective. We need to fight the urge to put important things off. We need to come to grips with our own mortality.

For this point, hand out paper and pencils and have everyone do the following math exercise. Explain that the Bible says, "Teach us to number our days aright, that we may gain a heart of wisdom" (Psalm 90:12). Tell everyone to (1) assume a life span of 80 years, (2) subtract their current age from 80, and (3) multiply that number by 365. The result is the approximate number of days they have left to live (if they don't die prematurely).

4. START *making time/spending time wisely*

- We need to decide what matters, what is important, and what we want to have accomplished when, at age 65, we look back on our lives.
- We must learn to distinguish between the important and the unimportant. And we must remember two facts:
  a. "I don't have time" means "I refuse to make time." We always have time for the activities we really want to do!
  b. Think carefully about time expenditures. Unlike any other commodity, time—once it is spent—is gone forever!

5. START *finding time*

- We each have 24 hours in a day. Some people accomplish much more than others because they spend their allotted time doing what matters most, not whatever feels good.
- Read Colossians 3:17.

ACTION

(5 min.)

Sharing

Return to the small groups. Give everyone the opportunity to share what they can do this week to change their schedule and reduce their stress level. Have them answer the following question: **What do you believe God wants you to do with your time?**

Have the groups pray together for each person in their small group, especially during the times they feel stress.

ACTIVE BONUS

"Balloon Shave"

Inflate and tie several balloons. Pick three boy-girl couples, and have the boys hold the ends of the balloons in their mouths. Cover the balloons with shaving cream. Give straight razors to the three girls, who race to "shave" all of the shaving cream off the balloon in their partner's mouth. Remember to inflate the balloons fully for more explosive action. Give a prize to the winner and towels to the losers.

You Make the Call

Tina Overload
You rush in and say in a panic:

"Hello, my name is Tina Overload and I am late again. I'm always late! I hate this watch because it just reminds me how little time I have to get all my jobs done. I'm taking a full load at school. I work 25 hours during the weekend, and I'm a member of the drama club, the yearbook staff, and an aerobics class. I've got a great boyfriend, but we always seem so rushed—no time to talk. I'm supposed to help at the nursing home next week and go with my church group on a retreat this weekend. I still haven't asked my boss for time off. I think I'm going crazy—I'm late, I'm late—I've got to go."

Then you rush out.

Bobby Brainstrain
You enter, quiet, looking tired, carrying a book bag.

"Hi, I'm Bobby Brainstrain, does anyone have an aspirin? My head is killing me. I have two huge tests tomorrow, both advanced placement courses. I wish I could stay for your meeting, but my parents signed me up for an SAT coaching course. They say that if I don't score 1200, I will be falling short of my potential. They went crazy when I scored 1050 last year. They want me in a good college. I can't imagine four more years of study, study, study. Sometimes I wonder if I am learning anything. I just wish I could take off some time to relax, but my parents will kill me if my grades slip this quarter. Sorry, my ride is here . . ." He moves toward exit. "Where are my vocabulary cards?"

Exit.

Donny Disaster
You enter, limping, looking tense.

"Hi, I'm Donny Disaster. This has been some week! First, I took my eyes off the road just for a moment to check out some babes, and boom!—some old lady decided to stop her car in the middle of the road for no good reason. Last night I saw my girlfriend eating ice cream with some college guy. No big deal! But when I called her, she said she had been home all night. After all the money I've spent on her . . . Then I stubbed my toe going to the bathroom in the dark last night. It hurts so much. Now, this morning, I can't find my chemistry lab notebook. If that baby has been stolen, I'm dead meat. Oh (grabs stomach) my stomach has been hurting all morning. I've got to find some of those green tablets. Why is all this happening to me?"

Exit.

Where Does All The Time Go?

1. Calculate your use of time, filling in the hours you spend during a typical week in each activity. Note: the total cannot exceed 168 hours! Fewer hours indicates either wasted or unaccounted for time.

2. Mark areas of your life where you feel stress with an asterisk (*).

3. Mark areas of your life that are important to you with a plus (+).

Hours spent per week:

_____ Sleeping

_____ In meetings

_____ On the phone

_____ Volunteering

_____ At parties

_____ Shopping

_____ Reading

_____ Watching TV, videos, and movies

_____ Driving

_____ In class

_____ At church and Bible studies

_____ Hanging out with friends

_____ Hobbies/recreation

_____ Exercising

_____ Personal grooming

_____ Dating

_____ Bible reading, praying

_____ Thinking

_____ Working

_____ Studying

_____ Eating

TEN

Sparks Be Flyin'

KEY CONCEPT:	Managing stress from conflict with others
BIBLE PASSAGES:	Selected passages from Proverbs and other selected passages
OBJECTIVE:	As a result of this meeting, students will handle stress from conflicts.
MATERIALS CHECKLIST:	☐ Bibles ☐ Pencils or pens ☐ Rolls of toilet paper ☐ Cellophane tape ☐ Envelopes with sets of instructions for ''Bandage Wrap'' ☐ Paper ☐ Chalkboard and chalk or erasable-marker board and markers ☐ Copies of the ''Anti-Stress Scriptures'' worksheet Active Bonus ☐ String or tape ☐ Balled-up newspapers
JUNIOR HIGH/MIDDLE SCHOOL ADAPTATION:	This lesson is ideal for junior highers because it teaches a life skill—how to resolve conflicts. Junior-high students, especially seventh and eighth graders, are constantly embroiled in interpersonal conflicts with friends, family, other kids, etc. The lesson should work well as written: just keep the discussion brief and work through the Bible study *together,* not in small groups.

STARTER
(10 min.)

"Bandage Wrap"

This is a relay. Divide into three or four teams and have each team send a representative to the front of the room. Place a roll of toilet paper, a roll of cellophane tape, and an envelope of instructions next to each representative. The sets of instructions should be identical for all the teams, but the teams may perform them in whatever order they like. Explain that at your signal, the first person in each team should run to the front, pull out an instruction from his or her team's envelope, and bandage the team's representative according to the instructions. Note: each bandage is toilet paper wrapped around the injured area. Each bandage must encircle the injured area five times and then be secured with tape. Here are some bandaging instructions: right ankle, left wrist, right hand, forehead, right knee, left foot, right elbow, left bicep, neck.

The first team to complete all its instructions successfully wins.

Transition

Say something like: **What a fun starter that was and what a great thing to do: bandaging people's wounds. The problem today is that we seem to spend a lot of time *causing* wounds instead of healing them, even to people we love. As a result, we live in stress on the most intimate level—at home and at school. We can choose who we see as strangers, but we can't really pick our friends. And we are absolutely stuck with our family. So we must learn to resolve our conflicts and work through our stress or we will suffer constantly.**

STUDY
(20 min.)

Discussion

Explain that to help understand our conflicts and find solutions, you want to begin with a brief discussion. Then ask:

- **How do most students resolve conflicts with their friends? How do you?**
- **How do most students resolve conflicts with their families? How do you?**
- **What causes most of the conflicts among students and their friends?**
- **What causes most of the conflicts in students' families? (probably clashes with parents)**
- **Who usually wins those conflicts?**

Bible Study

Break into small groups of three to five. Tell them to look up the passages of Scripture listed on the "Anti-Stress Scriptures" worksheet (you can write the passages on the board or give a copy of the worksheet to each group) and then jot down ideas for dealing with conflict with their families and friends.

After a few minutes, bring the whole group back together and share ideas. Here are some possible answers for each passage:

Proverbs 11:12—hold your tongue to stop quarrels
Proverbs 15:1—speak softly to avoid arguments
Proverbs 15:18—keep your cool to stop fights
Proverbs 15:28—think before you speak
Proverbs 17:14—don't let quarrels begin
Proverbs 18:13—learn the facts before making a decision
Romans 12:18—try to be at peace with everyone
Galatians 5:16—follow the leading of the Holy Spirit
Galatians 5:22-23—allow the Holy Spirit to control you
Hebrews 12:14—stay out of quarrels and live right
James 1:19—listen carefully and speak just a little

CHALLENGE

(5 min.)

Talk To

Say something like: **We can learn and grow from the conflicts in our lives, or we can become bitter and hurt. And, we can avoid some conflicts all together.**

We will encounter conflicts, but there are solutions—we do not have to settle for unpleasant relationships. But in order for this to happen, someone has to be an agent of change, love, and forgiveness. If you are a Christian, God has called you to be that kind of person, just like Jesus, in a fractured and hurting world.

"Time to Split!"

Continue: **Lots of times when we run into a conflict situation, the temptation is to split! Well, surprise, surprise, I'm going to tell you to do just that! But SPLiT doesn't mean exactly what you think it does.**

Write SPLiT down the left side of the board, like this:

S
P
Li
T

Explain that S stands for STOP. Write TOP after the S, to spell STOP. **When a conflict arises between you and a family member or friend, it's crucial not to allow it to escalate. So close your mouth, unclench your fists, and pause for a moment. . . . STOP.**

Use that moment to PRAY. Write RAY next to the P so that it spells PRAY. **Quickly ask God—this doesn't have to be out loud—to keep you calm and to give you patience. God will honor your request.**

Then, before you say anything, LISTEN. Write STEN next to the LI that you wrote earlier to spell LISTEN. **Allow the other person to talk. And don't just hear his or her words—listen to what he or she is really saying. Find the truth in the person's comments.**

Finally, TELL the person how you feel. Write ELL next to the T to spell TELL. **Don't tell the person what a jerk he or she is. Don't tell him or her how wrong he or she is. Tell the person your feelings—no one can disagree with that.**

After you've tried the SPLiT method, you may find that you no longer have a conflict. However, if disagreement still exists—compromise. Suggest a middle ground that would be mutually agreeable to both sides.

ACTION
(10 min.)

Role Plays

Have students pair up with someone of the same gender and act out the following role plays using the "SPLiT, then COMPROMISE" method. Designate the younger member of each pair as Person A and the other one as Person B.

- Person A, a high school junior, has just asked to borrow the car and has been told by his parent (Person B) that he/she can't have it because he/she has been out too many nights in a row. Start by getting mad at each other; then Person A should shift into the "SPLiT, then COMPROMISE" method.

- Person A and Person B are friends. Person A just learned that Person B has been seeing A's boyfriend/girlfriend. The role play starts with A shouting: "I can't believe you'd do this to me!" And B quickly responding, "What's your point?" Then B should use the "SPLiT, then COMPROMISE" method.

After the role plays are over, say: **Do the following things before the next week is over. I am sure that you will have the chance.**

- **Refuse to say a hurtful remark that could start a conflict.**
- **Refuse to spread a tidbit of gossip.**
- **Refuse to squabble over a petty matter.**

Prayer

Pray as a group for God to give strength as they go into the world as reconcilers rather than accusers.

ACTIVE BONUS

"World War III"

Divide the room in half with a piece of string or tape. Put half the group on each side of the room. Pile balled-up newspaper on each side, about 10 balls per person. At a signal have them begin throwing paper (one ball at a time) to the opposite side of the room. Half of each team should concentrate on offense (throw balls only) and half on defense (bat paper back to the other side).

After three minutes, have them stop. The team with the least paper on their side is the winner!

Anti-Stress Scriptures

The Scripture	The Anti-Stress Technique
Proverbs 11:12	
Proverbs 15:1	
Proverbs 15:18	
Proverbs 15:28	
Proverbs 17:14	
Proverbs 18:13	
Romans 12:18	
Galatians 5:16	
Galatians 5:22-23	
Hebrews 12:14	
James 1:19	

ELEVEN

Ex-cel-lennnt!

KEY CONCEPT:	Managing stress from the pressure to succeed
BIBLE PASSAGES:	Selected passages
OBJECTIVE:	As a result of this meeting, students will learn how to set realistic goals for themselves.
MATERIALS CHECKLIST:	☐ Bibles ☐ Pencils or pens ☐ Writing paper and envelopes ☐ Chalkboard and chalk or erasable-marker board and marker ☐ Copies of the ''Stress Test'' worksheet ☐ Copies of the ''Stress Rest'' worksheet
JUNIOR HIGH/MIDDLE SCHOOL ADAPTATION:	Early adolescents certainly are not immune to stress, so this topic is very relevant. Use the lesson as written with the following changes: after ''Stress Test'' keep the discussion concise; for Study, instead of breaking into small groups, work through the ''Stress Rest'' worksheet together. Also, don't use ''Better and Better'' with junior highers.

STARTERS
(10 min.)

"Stress Test"

Hand out pencils or pens and copies of the "Stress Test" worksheet. Give students nine minutes to perform as many of the items on the handout as possible.

Then, ask if anyone was able to complete the list. It is unlikely that anyone will have. Note: the answers to number 7 are: TIME, SCHEDULE, and PRESSURE.

Then discuss:

- **How did you feel trying to do everything?** (Probably stressed out.)
- **Did you enjoy this exercise? Why or why not?** (No—too stressful.)
- **In what ways is this exercise like your life?** (I do a lot of things and I'm not sure why. And in all of them, I'm trying to succeed, yet I often don't.)
- **In what specific ways or areas do you feel the pressure to excel?** Take time to get several answers.
- **Where does this pressure come from?** (Probably parents, teachers, coaches, and friends.)
- **When do you enjoy being pushed to excel, and when do you not enjoy it?** See what students say. Pressure to excel itself does not cause stress—many people enjoy pressure to excel as long as they have some confidence that success is possible. (This is true in most sports, for example.) Rather, pressure to excel becomes a source of stress whenever people feel overloaded or lack confidence that they can succeed. (This is true in sports whenever the game is a lost cause, for example.)

STUDY
(15 min.)

"Stress Rest"

Cut the "Stress Rest" worksheet into three sections. Break into small groups of four to six students and distribute a section to each group. (If you have more than three groups, photocopy the page so you have enough.) Have students take turns reading the passages aloud and discussing the questions. Give them five minutes.

After time's up, discuss what they learned. Here are some possible answers, but let the students do the talking:

- **What do these verses say about striving for excellence?** (We should strive for excellence—2 Corinthians 13:11; Philippians 3:14; Colossians 3:23.)
- **What do these verses say about God's desires for us?** (He does not want us to be stressed out; He wants us to have His peace and leave success with Him.)
- **How can a person work hard and strive for excellence, and yet be relaxed?** (By giving your concerns to God—1 Peter 5:7; Philippians 4:6-7)
- **In your life, when have you felt tense and pressured despite working extremely hard?**

CHALLENGE

(5 min.)

Talk To

Bring the group back together and say something like: **Does God want us to do our best? No doubt about it. Does God want us to worry about success? Absolutely not.**

One of the toughest parts of the Christian life is to strive for excellence and yet trust God to bring it. God wants you to strive, but not to worry.

Read the following passage to your students. Explain that it is part of a message that Moses gave to the people of Israel just before they entered the Promised Land. They felt the pressure to succeed and also were afraid they might *not* succeed.

Here's what Moses said to them: "When you go to war against your enemies . . . do not be afraid. . . . Do not be fainthearted or afraid; do not be terrified or give way to panic before them. For the Lord your God is the one who goes with you to fight for you against your enemies to give you victory" (Deuteronomy 20:1, 3-4 NIV).

Summarize: **The pressure for success isn't on you; it's on God! Your obligation is simply to "go to war." All you have to do is your part. Just do your best and walk with God. It's up to God to "give you victory."**

ACTION

(15 min.)

"Excellent!"

Write the following list of phrases on the board, and have the group define them. Don't judge their answers; just write what they say. Then go back and decide if they think anyone could ever realistically live up to these definitions. If not, redefine the phrases.

- an excellent student
- an excellent son or daughter
- an excellent athlete
- an excellent Christian
- an excellent friend
- an excellent employee
- an excellent boyfriend or girlfriend

Then discuss the following questions briefly:

- **Can a person be excellent in all these areas? If not, which ones?**
- **What does it mean to be a "driven person?"**
- **How do expectations affect the stress in your life?**
- **What unrealistic expectations do you have for yourself?**

Afterward, pass out sheets of paper and pencils or pens. Have students write themselves a letter about the ways that they have been too demanding of themselves and how they plan to change their attitudes and actions so that they can trust God, do their best, and not worry.

Have kids fold the letter, seal it in an envelope that you've provided, and address the envelope to themselves. Collect the letters and mail them to your students in a week or two.

Close in prayer.

ACTIVE BONUS

"Better and Better"

Seat everyone in a circle (or several circles if you have a large group). Give everyone a pencil or pen and a hard surface to write on. Explain that you will be distributing papers with the beginning of a situation or story at the top. When someone gets one of the sheets of paper, he or she should add one phrase or sentence to the situation to improve it. Then the person should pass the paper to the right and wait for the next paper. Here are some possible beginnings to the stories:

● John's car . . .
● On Celeste's research paper . . .
● Travis started at Defensive End in the biggest game . . .
● "There's a sale at the mall!" exclaimed Megan . . .
● Peter's relationship with Heather . . .
● The baseball team . . .

After they've added at least five phrases or sentences, collect the papers and read them aloud.

Stress Test

1. Do 25 sit-ups.

2. Add the following numbers: 888 + 75 + 1,453 + 6,239 + 136 + 212,091 + 8 + 16,874 =

3. Run around the perimeter of the room 5 times.

4. Get ten signatures from ten different people.

5. Write a four-line poem on the back of this sheet using the words "tarantula," "plastic," "couch," and "running." Make sure it rhymes.

6. Take off your shoes, do 20 jumping jacks, and then put your shoes back on.

7. Unscramble these letters to form words related to stress:

M E I T   D H E S C L E U   E R U P S E S R

___ ___ ___ ___   ___ ___ ___ ___ ___ ___ ___ ___   ___ ___ ___ ___ ___ ___ ___ ___

8. Find someone else with a picture of his or her mom or dad. Have that person sign here:

   _____

9. Comb or brush your hair and ask a friend how you look.

10. Read Exodus 18:13-27 and answer two questions:
    a. Who are the main people in this passage?

    b. What happened in this passage?

Stress Rest

Proverbs 12:24   2 Corinthians 13:11   Philippians 3:14   Colossians 3:23
Proverbs 3:5-6   Matthew 6:28-34   Philippians 4:6-7   1 Peter 5:7

- What do these verses say about striving for excellence?

- What do these verses say about stressing out?

- How can a person work hard and strive for excellence and yet be relaxed?

- In your life, when did you feel tense and pressured despite working extremely hard?

Proverbs 12:24   2 Corinthians 13:11   Philippians 3:14   Colossians 3:23
Proverbs 3:5-6   Matthew 6:28-34   Philippians 4:6-7   1 Peter 5:7

- What do these verses say about striving for excellence?

- What do these verses say about stressing out?

- How can a person work hard and strive for excellence and yet be relaxed?

- In your life, when did you feel tense and pressured despite working extremely hard?

Proverbs 12:24   2 Corinthians 13:11   Philippians 3:14   Colossians 3:23
Proverbs 3:5-6   Matthew 6:28-34   Philippians 4:6-7   1 Peter 5:7

- What do these verses say about striving for excellence?

- What do these verses say about stressing out?

- How can a person work hard and strive for excellence and yet be relaxed?

- In your life, when did you feel tense and pressured despite working extremely hard?

Will the Real Christians Please Stand?

KEY CONCEPT:	Managing stress from peer pressure
BIBLE PASSAGES:	Selected passages
OBJECTIVE:	As a result of this meeting, students will learn some ways to resist peer pressure.
MATERIALS CHECKLIST:	☐ Bibles ☐ Pencils or pens ☐ Signs that say, ''Absolutely Not!'' and ''You Better Believe It!'' (optional)
JUNIOR HIGH/MIDDLE SCHOOL ADAPTATION:	Peer pressure is a problem for almost all young people. Junior highers are beginning to feel its effects, so this meeting is very relevant. Use all three passages in ''Bible Search,'' but move through them quickly to get to the main points concerning peer pressure. Under Action, don't break into four parts; instead, brainstorm answers to the questions as a whole group.

STARTER
(5 min.)

"Would You?"

Explain that there is an imaginary scale (1 to 10) across the front of the room. One, at the left side of the room, represents "Absolutely not!" Ten, at the right side of the room, represents "You better believe it!" (You may wish to write these phrases on poster board and hang them up so that they are visible throughout the game.)

Tell students that they should stand in the appropriate place on the scale to indicate how they would react in each situation that you will read aloud. Give this example: "I would swallow a live goldfish." If students aren't sure how they would respond, have them stand in the middle where the number five would be on the invisible scale. Let them practice with this example. Answer any questions. Make sure that everyone understands how the game is played. Then read aloud each of the following statements one at a time, and let students respond to each.

- I would yell at a referee or an official while watching a game.
- I would go to the movies early to see the previews.
- I would tell a friend that he or she has bad breath.
- I would cover my eyes in a scary movie.
- I would get embarrassed if the topic of sex came up.
- I would go on a blind date.
- I would root for the underdog.
- I would stop and ask directions if I were lost.
- I would have cosmetic surgery.
- I would lie about my age.
- I would take my own refreshments into a movie.
- I would go skinny-dipping.
- I would ask the waitress or waiter to take my cold food and bring me food that is hot.

STUDY
(20 min.)

Discussion

Because students will be reluctant to take a strong stand on a number of these statements and will tend to look at what others do before they commit, discuss these questions:

- **Why is it sometimes difficult to say what you would do?** (Fear of being the only one, of being branded weird, or of being made fun of.)
- **When is it toughest to take a stand for what you truly believe?** (When no one else supports you, or when even your friends fail to support you.)
- **How do you feel when you're not sure what to do?** (Probably nervous, anxious, or even isolated.)
- **How do you make decisions when you don't know how you feel about certain situations?** (Probably see what everyone else is doing.)
- **What are convictions?** (Strong beliefs about what is right.)

Bible Search

Have a student read the following verses aloud. After each set of verses is read, discuss the questions that go with it.

94

1. Numbers 13:1-3; 25-31; 14:1-10a

- **What was the situation in this passage?** (Moses sent spies into Canaan to see what the land was like; they reported their findings.)
- **What did the majority of the spies say?** (The people shouldn't invade Canaan because the land was filled with giants.)
- **Who did the people listen to? Why?** (They listened to the majority of the spies because they were afraid.)
- **How would you have felt if you were Caleb?**
- **How would you have reacted if you had been in the crowd of people listening to these reports?**

2. John 12:37-43

- **Why were some people afraid to stand up for (or publicly follow) Jesus?** (They were afraid of the religious leaders.)
- **What stresses do we encounter because of our faith?** (Opposition or scorn from friends and other peers.)
- **When is it good or bad to want people to like you?** (It's good if you want them to like you for being good; it's bad if you want them to like you at all costs.)
- **What are the dangers of wanting to be accepted?** (The danger is that you'll sacrifice something you shouldn't in order to be accepted.)
- **Why is it helpful to have some close friends who share your belief in Christ?** (They can back you up in your commitment to Christ.)

3. Acts 4:8-20

- **Why was Peter able to be so bold?** (He had been with Jesus and was filled with the Holy Spirit.)
- **Put yourself in Peter and John's place. How do you think you might have responded if some authority told you to quit talking about Jesus?**
- **In what ways do your friends or classmates pressure you to keep quiet about your faith?**
- **In what ways do your friends or classmates discourage you from doing what is right?**

CHALLENGE

(2 min.)

Talk To

Say something like: **You will experience stress whenever others pressure you to do what is wrong or not do what is right. That's part of being a Christian. Sitting here, it's easy to feel that you could never abandon the truth. But when you get in situations that pressure you to compromise, only solid convictions will see you through. I just want to tell you that it's worth standing your ground. Many of your friends wish they were so courageous.**

Let's spend some time now looking at how to develop strong convictions.

ACTION
(15 min.)

Brainstorm

Divide into four groups and have each group brainstorm answers to one of these questions or issues:

- **How can the Bible help us develop strong convictions?** (It can show us what God wants us to do and the rewards of following God's will.)
- **How can Christian friends hold us accountable when peer pressure strikes?** (They can encourage us to be strong and remind us of God's Word.)
- **What can Christian kids do (if anything) to stop tempting situations from being quite so tempting?** (They can ask God for strength to resist and remember that God's way is best.)
- **Why is the desire to be accepted so strong?** (Everyone wants to be liked by others.)

After about 10 minutes, bring everyone back together and have the groups report their findings.

Prayer

Close with a time of silent prayer. Encourage kids to talk to God about the situations they are facing in which they feel pressured to compromise the truth.

ACTIVE BONUS

"Stand Ups"

Have everyone be seated on the floor. Tell them to stand if the statement you read applies to them.

- Stand up if you hate to stand out from the crowd.
- Stand up if you would rather be somewhere else.
- Stand up if it was entirely your choice to be here.
- Stand up if you like (that is, have a romantic interest in) somebody here. Remain standing if it's me.
- Stand up if you believe in standing up for what you believe.
- Stand up if you think you can believe sitting down.
- Stand up if you feel foolish just sitting there.
- Sit down if you want us to go on to something else.

ADDITIONAL IDEAS

"Common Bond"

Give each student a copy of the following list, and a pencil or pen. Have them go through the group getting signatures from different people for each of the categories. Each person can only sign each list once.

- I share your birth month
- I am in the same grade

- I live in the same neighborhood or complex
- I have the same kind of pet
- I like the same musical group(s) as you
- I have the same name (first, last, or middle)
- I like the same kind of dessert
- I enjoy the same hobby or pastime
- I am in the same mood right now (happy, sad, laid back, apathetic, stressed, angry)
- I have the same favorite color

Video

Show part of the movie "Zelig," the story of a man who goes to any lengths to fit in. See the book *Video Movies Worth Watching* (Baker, 1992) for ideas on how to use this video.

JOIN THE
REVOLUTION

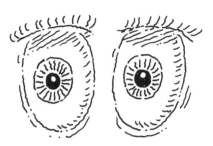

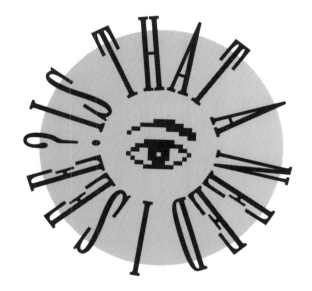

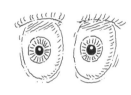

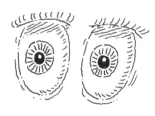

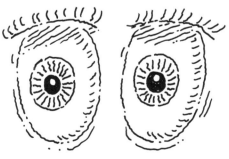

Is That a Need I See?

OUTWARD BOUND!

OUTWARD BOUND!

Outward Bound!

You Gotta Get These Gifts

PUT YOUR BEST FOOT FORWARD

OPPORTUNITY KNOCKS

CHARLES SCHLOB—NOT

CHARLES SCHLOB—NOT

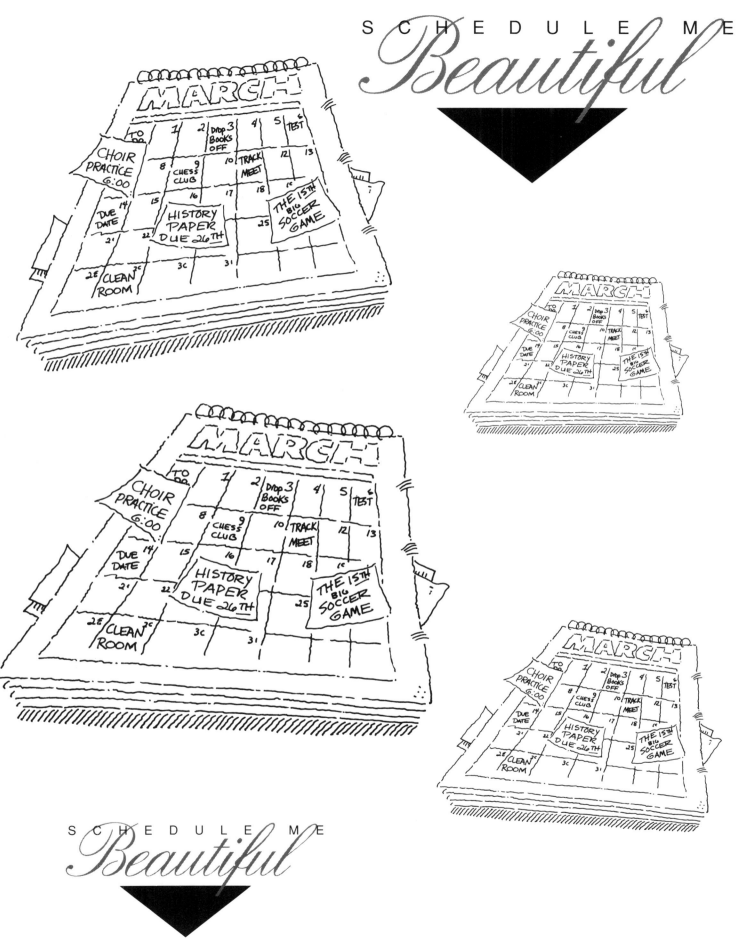

Schedule Me Beautiful

SPARKS BE FLYIN'

EX-CEL-LENNT!

WILL THE REAL CHRIST IAN PLEASE STAND UP?